Giftus has a gift, and sharing it is horiter, poet and family man. Wow! He soldier... n his very early work, which appeared in the S... his last novel, *Ma William and Her Circle of F*... excitement. He has presented us with culturally roote... stories and poetry, connected to our beloved Dominica; yet interesting enough, to be widely read.

Verses from atop the Mountain, takes us to a higher height—the mountain top. A must read collection of poetry which touches on politics, nostalgia, and pertinent questions such as, "Where Are The Children?" sprinkled with a few Japanese style Haiku, which deserve a place in the collection, Giftus takes us on a sweet ride. Amidst the lamentation of "foreign" living, such as "The Migrant's Song," we are treated to some soft tender moments: "Your Shadow," and "The Last Dance"—a sweet, rhythmic movement.

Giftus has done it again! Every poem here can be honorably mentioned. *Verses from atop the Mountain*: a litany of reasons he is not "here". For:

> *"I am here because I am me*
> *I am here because he set me free*
> *I am here because there is hope."*

Indeed, Giftus gives us hope with *Verses from atop the Mountain.*

Lionel "*Les Li*" Leslie...*Dominica Poetic Circle.*

The title, "*Verses from atop the Mountain*," immediately conveys a sense of peace, away from the fray. This new collection of poems, by Giftus John, invites his readers to partake of his meditative sojourn atop, and away from the valley of distraction, and our own busy life. As, is his flair, Giftus provides a universal array of thought and feeling, while sitting you, softly, yet firmly, into his homeland.

The idiosyncrasy and colloquial flavor of Giftus' island of origin, Dominica, blends in with themes and topics, global and common. By the last line, of the last verse, of the last poem, we, readers, find ourselves atop that same mountain, giving air and moment to thoughts, too often glanced over in our hustle and bustle. Poetry has the transformative ability to allow us such escape, and Giftus adeptly provides a multitude of outlets to attend, with him, atop the mountain, in this wonderful anthology of thoughtful reflections.

Kalinago Woryi

Verses from atop the Mountain

Reflections from the Heart of Waitukubuli

Also by Giftus:

The Island Man Sings His Song
Mésyé Kwik! Kwak!
Ma William and Her Circle of Friends

Verses from atop the Mountain

Reflections from the Heart of Waitukubuli

A COLLECTION OF POEMS

BY

GIFTUS R. JOHN

WITH A FOREWORD

BY

TED SERRANT PHD

VERSES FROM ATOP THE MOUNTAIN
REFLECTIONS FROM THE HEART OF WAITUKUBULI

Front Cover design, and other illustrations, by author.

iUniverse books may be ordered through booksellers or by contacting:

iUniverse
1663 Liberty Drive
Bloomington, IN 47403
www.iuniverse.com
1-800-Authors (1-800-288-4677)

ISBN: 978-1-4917-6053-6 (sc)
ISBN: 978-1-4917-6052-9 (e)

Library of Congress Control Number: 2015903133

Print information available on the last page.

iUniverse rev. date: 3/24/2015

Table of Contents

Foreword

Lotka's law posits that most people will write one article or one book in their lifetime. This, I believe, is Giftus' fourth anthology of poems. Giftus has defied the odds. He has been defying the odds for a long time. I know! He taught me years ago. I congratulate you on a provoking piece of work, and thank you for inviting me to present the forward for this anthology. I am honored that the teacher can turn it over to his student.

Verses from atop the Mountain, signals a proclamation, a call, and a cry. This proclamation is symbolized by both the verses and the location from which they are proclaimed. The mountains, therefore, are metaphors for heights attained and the universality of the messages embedded in these verses. They are also symbolic of Giftus' mountainous island origin and the land that remains almost like an unsettled bargain in these verses. "The Migrant Song" captures that unsettled existence derived from residence in an adopted homeland. Much of the work in this anthology, then, comes from lived experiences, a persistent banter between what is, and what used to be, what is left behind, and with what one now contends. In "The Land Beckons Me," he finds solace and the assurance that he is not a castaway confirming the temporariness of the migrant tension between the homeland and the adopted homeland.

The work is a "literary hopscotch" (and I mean it in a flattering way,) of themes that addresses love, nature, reality, expectations, dreams and ambitions lined with hope and restoration: "The Sun Rises Tomorrow;" "The Morning Awakens." This hopscotching, to me, is the art of a multifaceted artist, and Giftus is multifaceted. He is painter, writer, and poet. This book bears this out as he weaves together pieces on the spring, fall and the snow; things that are transient and yet in "Ode to a Tree Stump," he finds not just death, decay, and a break from the past, but endurance of that past. With its roots buried deeply, the stump remains as a lasting memory of its legacy. For him, the more things change the more they remain the same. That sentiment comes through in his serious treatises on politics and freedom, two of the things that vex us most.

This anthology traverses the human emotion as well: From an elusive love to solitude, nightmare, cowardice, and death—his mom's. Then almost in a 'tantalizing soliloquy,' he asked, "For whom does the church bell toll?" Despite the hopscotching, Giftus returns again and again to the theme of his beloved land and community, a microcosm of the returning nature of West Indian migration. In the end, he reckons that we all are cut form the same cloth. Simply, this anthology is all of us, reflects all of us, and speaks to all of us from the mountaintop. Listen!

Ted D. Serrant PhD
Senior Fellow
Rise Institute
Washington, DC

Introduction

I began my literary journey writing poetry when I was in my second year of high school at the St. Mary's Academy, in the capital city, Roseau. I did this to express my thoughts as a young fourteen year old, eager to let others know how I felt. I found it easy to put my thoughts on paper, and realized I was getting my message across based on the feedback I received from classmates and others who had read what I had written. This gave me the impetus to share my work in the local media, especially the Star Newspaper and DBS Radio, paving a path for my literary development.

I took a break from publishing poetry since the release of *The Island Man Sings His Song*, in 2001, yet I still made time to write. My poetry may not fall in line with what most people expect, but to me, expressing what I think and feel, is what matters.

Verses from atop the Mountain is a collection of poems that spans almost ten years. I have covered a variety of topics, and though most of the thoughts expressed seem personal, I believe I also express the thoughts of many on the topics that I have written.

I have entitled the book *Verses from atop the Mountain* for many reasons, one of which is that I believe that since a mountain is the highest point on the earth, and we all strive to get to the highest point in our everyday lives, I should strive to get to my own mountain. When we get to the top of our mountain, it means that we have accomplished a great milestone, even though we may have encountered setbacks along the way. Getting to the top allows us to forget the pain that we encountered along the journey. In the end, it is worth all that it took to get there.

I hope you find your journey to the top of the mountain a satisfying, fruitful, and worthwhile one, and when you get there, you will be able to enjoy the wonderful view that awaits you. I invite you to come along with me on my journey to the mountaintop.

Blessings!

Giftus

Acknowledgement

I give all the praise to the Almighty for having blessed me with the gifts and talents that I possess. Without him at my side, none of this would have been possible.

I want to express my gratitude to all who assisted with getting this book completed. It has been a team effort and each of you has played a role in the final product. I thank you for accepting my request to help in whatever way you could. I am aware that some of you had your own situations to deal with, yet you came forward and assisted, to make this book a reality. I take this opportunity to recognize, *Lionel "Les Li" Leslie, Ted Serrant, Ophelia Olivaccé-Marie, Lola Louis, Kalinago Woryi, and Eunice Nisbett.*

I would also like to thank my wife Theresa, my children, and my family in Dominica, for their continued support.

Thanks again, each of you, and my sincerest appreciation for your help, support, and cooperation. As Ted so rightly states, *"This anthology is all of us, reflects all of us, and speaks to all of us..."*

Love!

Geejay

Dedication

I dedicate this collection
To my daughter Mandisa and my son Jamal,
And to all the children
Of my home village,
St. Joseph.

****

The playground is still:
No sounds, no cries,
Of children,
Running to and fro.

The Village Awakens

Dawn breaks quietly
As birds welcome the morning
With their cacophony of songs.
The trees stand quietly in respect
As the sun edges purposefully
Over the dark-green mountains,
Its resplendent rays,
Bathing the land with its majesty.

The dew drops drip slowly
From the petals, unto the grass
Glistening in the sunlight,
As the plants, growing freely,
Welcome the new day,
Thankful for the warmth
Of the morning sun, as they
Proudly display their beauty.

The red-crested humming birds,
With long, pointed beaks,
Hover menacingly above the flowers,
Their wings, flapping like rotors,
As they take aim
At the stamens,
Ready to siphon
The deep-seated nectar.

Hens, with their broods
Close in pursuit,
Cluck noisily and defiantly,
As they scurry about
Hunting for careless worms
Before the robins and wrens do,
While ignoring the advances
Of the colorful, persistent roosters.

The bees and wasps
Buzz and hum, noisily,
As they quickly dart about
Feasting on the abundant pollen.
Yet, it is calm and peaceful,
Even as the river, briskly flows,
Meandering its way to the Caribbean Sea,
As the morning quietly hearkens.

The glistening fronds
Of the giant palm trees
Lay limp and listless,
Fearful to disturb the morning with their rustle.
And, as I watch from my window,
I smile in awe
At the beauty being unveiled around me,
As the village, too, awakens.

I Saw You Last Night

I saw you last night
Under the silvery moonlight
My loving arms around you,
As I whispered softly in your ears.
I tried calming your fears
Yet, you sobbed softly.
A frog croaked loudly
As I gently wiped away your tears.

I held you tenderly
As the full moon slid silently
Across the starry night,
And an owl hooted mockingly, nearby.
I felt your throbbing heart
With my trembling hands
As your chest heaved
With each, deep, painful sigh.

I kissed you slowly,
Enjoying every single moment,
Under the twinkling stars,
As we lovingly embraced each other.
Too scared to let go,
We said nothing for a while
But stood still in the moonlight
Wishing that moment would last forever.

But you are gone today
For I see no trace of you.
Yet, I keep yearning to hold you again,
Even as my aching head throbs.
In vain, I stretch out my arms
But, no one embraces me.
The moon no longer shines as brightly
Even as I hear the echo, of your distant sobs.

I saw you last night
As you mesmerized me.
Yes my dear, I saw you,
More beautiful than ever before.
You stood beside my bed
Painfully tantalizing me,
Your eyes fixed on my beaten frame,
Even as you walked out the door.

I shed some tears, my dear,
As I remembered the moments
We shared together, in the shadows
Of the giant breadfruit trees.
I saw you, my once beloved,
As we strolled slowly at midnight
Along the soft, sandy shore,
Enjoying the cool evening breeze.

I am awake now.
It would have been better
If I were still asleep,
For it pains, so much to see you leave.
Yet, I will always be haunted
By the words you whispered, in my ears,
Before you turned and walked away,
Leaving me to pine and grieve.

Ode To A Tree Stump

Look at you now, poor thing,
A mere reminder of what you once were
Along this busy Union thoroughfare;
Now slowly fading away into oblivion.

Once maybe, a thing of beauty,
A tree of great pride, I dare say,
Adored by all who laid eyes on you
As you offered relief from the noonday sun.

What can you now say for yourself?
For time, as you know it would,
Has finally caught up with you; sealing your fate,
Just as happened to many others, around this town.

Oh yes, you, this giant ugly stump,
Sure evidence of your past size and girth.
Maybe your branches, once upon a time,
Spread themselves out over this busy county street.

Standing firm with roots so deep
And branches reaching up to the sky,
You were a haven for birds, lizards, and squirrels,
That found you a safe place to rest, sleep, and eat.

Where, once a tired man, or woman,
Or, even a little child, sat for a while,
Beneath your branches on a hot summer's day,
As they took a moment to rest their weary feet.

Maybe even a four-legged friend or two
Sometimes found you a welcome sight,
Lifting their hind legs to relieve themselves
Because, to them, you were just another tree.

Back then, I am sure, you towered majestically,
Reaching up to the sky; dwarfing all around you.
Oh! What a sight you must have been then!
A joy, I may say, for everyone in Union to see.

For many years, you stood tall, resolute, and strong,
Daring the rain to fall and the winds to blow,
Or holding fast in the sleet, hail, or snow.
Sure, I can tell, you were once a tall, proud tree.

But look at you, once so strong and graceful,
Alas, but food for hungry bugs and worms;
A sanctuary for weevils, millipedes, and centipedes
While now, not even the dogs see any use for you.

Ah, poor thing, protruding from the ground:
Nothing but an annoying sight, rather than
The thing of beauty that you once were,
Right here, along this very busy, township avenue.

Fare thee well, great tree! Fare thee well!
Maybe someday, another shall fill this spot,
Or, maybe not! Just a thought or a dumb wish.
However, if one does, will it meet the same fate as you?

The Colors of Her Life

With various tones
Of ink
She paints her life
As she puts the pieces together
Punctuated with sloppy dabs
And loose, carefree strokes
Unto the stretched canvas,
Placed on the shaky easel before her.

Against a backdrop
Of pain, neglect, and hurt
She tells her story
Of abuse and fear.
A story, once fresh and vibrant,
Now chapped and peeling
Off the damaged canvas,
She now desperately tries to repair.

Once, a beautiful picture,
Now cracked and dull
As she continually attempts
To forget her plight and fate.
A single mom
Deceived, sad, lonely, and hurt,
She struggles to add brighter colors
To revive this now faded portrait.

Not too long ago,
She painted a beautiful picture
With warm, soothing hues,
Drawn with such delicate touch.
Each image, patiently sketched,
Clearly outlined and highlighted,
As she detailed her story;
One she now, sadly, has to retouch.

It is raining now
And the colors on the canvas,
Streak down slowly
In crooked, messy lines, before her,
As the raindrops wash away
The sad images forever,
Leaving her a blank canvas
And the chance for a makeover.

Solitude...*for my daughter, Mandisa*

Morning breaks slowly and quietly now
As the sun barely shines through the clouds.
Nothing at all seems to move about
Down here near this warm and quiet hut.
Inside, there is but peace, calm, and silence,
Save for the crackling wood fire.
And I look out towards the winding stream,
Just below the green sloping hills, then
Over to where the noisy water mill, now
Hidden by trees and shrubs, once churned. Yet,
Nothing stirs. Even the wind is quiet today.

I Wait For Spring

I long for the spring
Anxious to see what it will bring.
I long to smell the beautiful flowers
Nourished by the refreshing rain showers.

Like a child, I wait for the spring,
To fly my kite at the end of a string.
To watch it float effortlessly, way up high,
With the birds, in the blue noonday sky.

I patiently wait to see the spring:
To hear a chorus of happy birds sing,
As they hop merrily along, from tree to tree,
Hunting for bugs, nectar, or even a careless bee.

With bated breath I wait for the spring
To hear the sound of the rushing spring;
To watch beautiful flowers open before my eyes
Displaying life's simplicity and nature's precious prize.

I think I hear it coming around the corner.
Oh! How I wish it could get here much sooner,
For I will be happy and enthralled each day,
As the snow and the ice, slowly begin to melt away.

Let spring come on along, as she will.
Let her come and our empty lives to refill.
Let her come to replenish a cold and dreary earth
With her flora and fauna, signs of a new life and birth.

Soon, we will say bye to "ole man winter,"
Farewell to his cold winds and his chilly weather.
We will now begin to prepare the velvet carpet,
As spring, with her charm and beauty, we prepare to meet.

Yes, I will eagerly wait for you, spring
With all the magic that you will surely bring.
I will pray and wait patiently, as my time I bide,
Like the groom nervously awaiting his beautiful bride.

What Is Freedom?

What is freedom?
Is it the right
To engage
In whatever one wants,
Desires, or craves daily,
Whether it is, wrong or right?
Is freedom the choice
To quench the desires
Of the heart and body,
Or the right to speak one's mind,
Whether hurtful, insincere, or malicious.
Or said out of anger, or out of spite?

Is freedom
A need,
To hear lamenting and dissenting voices,
Demanding change
Yet not changing themselves,
As they wave accusing fingers, menacingly?
Soon, the blame game begins:
No one blames himself
For the morass we create,
The nightmares we grow,
The pain we cause others,
The fears we nurture daily.

We blame politicians
For our demise,
And our every deficiency,
While we traumatize and sodomize,
The vulnerable ones around us,
With hate, bitterness, and contempt.
We have become parodies
Of the racists and hatemongers,
Betraying our families and friends,
While smearing the good name
Of our brothers and sisters,
As we sow the seeds of resentment.

Is freedom
A call to bear arms?
Is it the choice to segregate?
To discriminate?
Is it the right to propagate
Civil disorder and corruption?
Yet, we squander and waste,
At the expense of
The sick, poor, and destitute
As we eradicate our very own,
Spilling innocent blood and
Silencing all who speak in opposition.

Is freedom
The right to portray ourselves
Like animals
Stampeding through the arid land
With no decency nor regard,
For ourselves and our very own?
Is it our callous disregard
For the sanctity and respect
Of our fellow brothers and sisters,
As we behave inhumanely:
Bloated with disdain as
Seeds of contempt, we have sown?

Is there a color to freedom?
Is it yellow or brown? White or black?
Is it the ability to curse our own kind
Yet glorify the sham
Of the stranger
Even though he is a fraud and miscreant,
A traitor, moonlighting as our savior,
Yet, watering the seeds of discourse
That they have planted
As the poisons course through our veins;
Stifling our cry for equality and fairness,
Forcing us to go silent?

Is freedom the yearning
To be, whom you are?
The yearning to be
Who you want to be, regardless?
Regardless of the nature
Of your situation?
Regardless of the price being paid
For the freedom you yearn
So dearly to have,
Yet, sadly, it is
Taken away, denied, gambled, or sold,
With no hope for restitution?

Is freedom the right
To choose between
Life and death; gay and straight,
Red, green, and blue,
Single, divorced, and married,
Good, indifferent, and evil?
Is freedom a choice
Between the Diaspora and Dominica?
Between a shoe, a saw, and a hand?
The *petit boug* and *gwo boug*?
The educated and foolish?
God and the devil?

What is freedom then?
Is it just a seven-letter word
Spewed from angry, saliva-filled mouths
Bellowing in anger,
Eyes ablaze with fury,
As they come rumbling into town
Expressing their envy and hate,
Enticing the angry ones to take up arms,
Rallying the ignorant and foolish,
To create mayhem, chaos, and discord
Yet, at the end of it all,
They are sadly demeaned and frowned upon?

After all their selfless sacrifices
The masses remain locked out
In the dark and the cold,
Aimlessly gazing
At darkened windows with blinds drawn,
Testing their desire and resolve.
In vain, they await the rewards
The politicians promised.
In vain, they await the freedom
They've fought and died for,
But now, slowly disappearing,
Like the thin clouds, skimming above.

What is Freedom?

Birds, Bees and Buds

The bud has sprouted
Drawing to her
Birds and bees
Lured by her sweet smell.

Your Shadow

I see you walk past
Everyday,
Hurrying along,
Your head held high;
Your eyes unflinching,
Daring me
To shout your name,
As I stand gazing and wishing.

I watch you
As you stroll along,
Purposefully:
Your hair, black and long;
Your lips, supple and inviting
Bearing a warm, seductive smile
As you glide along
On this beautiful Sunday evening.

I watch silently,
From my window,
As I fondly yearn
To embrace you.
Yet, I wait patiently for my turn
As you toy with
Prospective lovers,
Staring at you with profound admiration.

I watch you walk by,
Always so confident;
Your tall, beautiful, and womanly figure,
Gracefully shown,
Shaped and modeled,
By the hand of the Creator
As my bleeding heart races
Uncontrollably, in sheer anticipation.

My body shivers
As you walk along
In the warm golden rays
Of the setting sun;
Your thin shadow,
Stretching out to the front of my door.
I pray fervently,
Hoping the image I see is true.

I yearn to hold you.
I long to squeeze you and
Feel the sensuous pulsations,
Of your warm body,
Thump lovingly
Against my aching frame
As if a *lapo kabwit* drum
Reverberates deep within you.

I feel the emotions
Rushing wildly within us
And the sweat
Oozing slowly,
Lubricating our young,
Warm and tender bodies,
As we eagerly savor
These romantic moments together.

Yet, I watch
As you smile mockingly;
As your shimmering image
Haunts my fogged mind.
I turn and roll,
My eyes, wide open,
As this lonely, painful night,
Slowly grows even longer.

I sing my song:
A sad painful one.
I watch hopelessly,
In despair,
As the flower that I admire
Quickly wilts away
Before I have the pleasure
To appreciate the wonderful view.

I quietly ask myself
"What if?"
"What if, my dear?"
I whisper agonizingly,
As the pain courses through my body,
Wondering if I could get
Just that one chance, again!
To tell you how much I love you.

The Bell Tolls

I hear the knell of the church's bell.
For whom it tolls, I do not know,
Yet it is a sad story, it sure does tell
Of a fellow villager, we all did know.

I hear the knell and I say a prayer
As I look towards the misting hills.
Someone, at this moment, sure sheds a tear,
For another sad moment, the village feels.

The elder folk for a moment pause,
As to a dear friend they say so long.
Yet, as they mourn that person's loss,
Today, in the village, life still moves along.

For there is a cry of joy, amid the pain,
Even as the sexton continues to ring the bell
Sounding again and again, the sad refrain,
That someday, another shall ring for him, as well.

For across the street, on this early morn,
The village midwife tends to a mother
Who, this day, gave birth to a son:
Now, another poor soul depends on her.

Surely life's cycle, as it always does,
Continues for both the rich and poor.
For even as the villagers mourn their loss,
There is hope, as new life abounds next door.

The bell grows quiet as it begins to rain
Yet, it is calm and peaceful inside the room.
Outside, there is sorrow, sadness and pain,
As we share in both the happiness and the gloom.

Until Dawn Arrives

The wind howls loudly.
Inside, we are scared
To move
Until dawn arrives.

Truant

Inside, teachers and pupils
Are busy at work
But on the steps of the village school,
Under the shelter of the large eave,
A young boy sits alone,
Openly defying the principal's rule.

The raindrops fall to the ground
Splattering before him
As he sucks at the end of a *ti bum* stick
Dipping it again and again
In the bottle held between his legs
Like he has done every day this week.

His dirty face displays a sign of joy,
Freedom, contentment, and fearlessness
As a drop of what he eats
Falls unto his blue shirt.
Yet another stain appears
That will surely test his mother's wits.

The succulent berries, he has picked,
Filling his bottle to its narrow neck
And with a little bit
Of brown sugar, secretly taken
From his mother's safe,
He has made himself his *meewees* treat.

Slowly, he bends the bottle
Into his already stained mouth
Sucking out the last, juicy bits,
As he swings his mud-covered legs
Back and forth; quite relaxed,
Playfully spitting out the useless pits.

His folded exercise book
He has placed in his pocket.
His pencil...lost somewhere
During his long *meewees* hunt.
Lessons are now the last thing,
About which this truant wants to hear.

The brew is all but finished now
As he ponders the next move.
Undaunted by his absence at roll call
He is in no hurry to get to class
As he wipes his red stained hands
Along the newly painted wall.

He is satisfied now:
Seemingly at peace with himself.
And, as if by some compelling power,
He strolls through the classroom door,
Nonchalantly, looking about,
As his classmates alert the teacher.

But does he really care?
With bottle and stick in his back pocket;
A contented heart and a full stomach,
He will patiently sit and bide his time.
For when that final bell rings at three,
To *Yard* he will go right back.

Sunlight

It is dry again
Though the rain
Fell unceasingly
Throughout the night.

Cut From the Same Cloth

They are all the same
Wearing disguises and
Showing phony smiles
As they come playing their games;
Their devious plans they want us to approve
Yet in the end, they leave us empty-handed.

They all come,
Knocking hard and repeatedly,
At our front doors,
As they come answering the call
To create and spread hatred and jealousy,
Among the hapless, ignorant, and poor.

They promise us everything,
While fabricating untrue stories
With their forked tongues.
Yet, after all this, we gain nothing
But hurt, pain, deception, and heartaches
As a fooled people, sing their mournful songs.

Robed like the Magi
They come, quietly by night,
In the cold and the dark.
They stare at us with deceiving eyes,
Pretending to feel sorry for our plight
Yet truthfulness and honesty, they all surely lack.

Like Eden's serpent
They entrap us all
With bogus plans and frivolous schemes,
Promising us money, jobs, and development,
Until, from their lofty perches, they all fall,
Crippling a nation's hopes and its dreams.

From the Middle East to Dominica
They quickly evolve,
Desolate men wanting control and power.
From Capuchin to Scotts Head; Layou to Salybia,
Simple problems they cannot even resolve
Yet they get richer and the people grow poorer.

They are all the same
Spreading seeds of hate and malice,
While encouraging wastefulness and bribery.
They chase power, money, and fame
As they encourage greed, anger, and injustice;
Creating a culture of fear, distrust, and misery.

Like nocturnal beasts,
They come
Searching for vulnerable prey.
They come, creating morose and squalor,
While my beloved country they keep fleecing,
Upholding immorality as the order of the day.

Oh! Where have they gone?
The noble and decent men!
Men of integrity, substance, and vision?
Oh! What have we done,
With those who cared about our children's future,
Unlike those bent on destroying our island nation?

With hateful tongues and hurtful words
We scarred them all.
Today, only the rogues and their lackeys remain,
Since we chased away the honest ones
Who dared not answer the battle cry
For *mepuis*, hypocrisy, injustice, and illicit gain.

Whether black or white,
Blue, green, or red,
They are all the same
As they cling to power for all it's worth,
Jailing, killing, and maiming, their very own
While men of honor and integrity they defame.

For money, power and for fame
They ride on the weak backs
Of the poor, misguided, and ignorant souls.
However, they are all the same
Despots, dictators, power hungry maniacs,
Destroying and pilfering, like desperate ghouls.

Nevertheless, they are alike,
Even if they change their tunes and colors.
Whether from north, south, east or west
Our anger and resolve, they try to tame.
Our welfare, they take for-granted,
While the call, for change and honesty, they detest.

So Soon!

I did not get a chance to say goodbye
Nor a chance to hold your hand.
I did not get a moment
To reminisce one more time
For it happened so quickly
As you departed this world,
When the call from heaven came,
And the angels carried you away.

My heart sank, as reality struck.
So soon! So quick!
"Why so fast?" I wondered aloud.
However, I was powerless,
For your Lord had summoned you,
And obediently,
You answered his call,
Closing your eyes forever that day.

A sad farewell dear Mother.
A sad and sudden end
To a life of love and devotion,
Gentleness and tenderness.
But who am I to question
What the Lord orders?
Who am I to question his plan,
As he called you home that afternoon?

Fare thee well, dear Mother!
Nevertheless, fear not,
For we'll keep the flowers blooming;
We will keep your smile alive
As we remember you
Your watchful eyes always on us
As we ran about
In the sun, or in the light of the moon.

Heaven awaits you, dear Mother
And the angels
Will welcome you home
With the joyful sound
Of their trumpets.
The saints will rejoice,
As you join the choirs of angels,
Praising your Father in song.

With your gentle, loving hands,
You will tend
To the flowers growing freely
In Heaven's gardens.
The birds too,
Will chirp happily
As they fly from branch to branch
Keeping you company all day long.

Where Are The Children?

The playgrounds are quiet.
The ballparks,
Now overgrown with weeds,
Used as pasture for cattle.
The swings and benches,
Where they once played,
Are dilapidated,
Broken and beyond repair.

Where are the children?

The fruits ripe and fall,
From the over-laden branches,
Lying in heaps
As they rot on the ground.
They remain untouched
Except by the birds and lizards,
Thankful for the bountiful crop
Going to waste everywhere.

Where are the children?

The classrooms are empty.
Troubled teachers patiently await
The absent students
To occupy the benches.
The church is almost empty.
Only the elderly occupy
The wooden pews,
As the aging pastor struggles on.

Where are the children?

The village is quiet
As the sun eases
Towards the distant horizon,
Casting long shadows
Upon the once alive and vibrant village,
Abuzz with children at play,
As they ran about having fun.

Lord! Where are the children?

No *timtims* are being told.
No *mésyé kwik! kwak!*
No ring games played,
No *lawan*…nothing!
As the moon looks on sadly
From the starry sky,
Patiently waiting for the children,
To play in its light.

But, where are the children?

Where are the children?
We cry aloud
As we pray fervently
On aching knees.
We raise our tired hands aloft
Looking up to the mountains,
Pleading unceasingly,
Before we go to sleep tonight.

Where are the children?

So I, too, ask again.
Where are the children?
As I watch the flowers wilt away
Now useless to the bees.
Where are our children?
I cry aloud
As the warm raindrops
Now begin to fall.

Where are the children?

Another sad end,
To a once beautiful day
As the night insects hiss loudly,
From their places of refuge.
The leaves
Of the mango trees rustle
As if echoing
Our sad and painful call.

Where are the children?

The River

It looks calm and still
But it swiftly
Flows along,
Heading to the sea.

The Scars Remain

He keeps muttering
The questions she had asked
As she wipes away the tears
That stream down her still beautiful face.
He searches for answers
As he witnesses her sorrow.
He feels the guilt
As he watches her sad and painful grimace.

He stands motionless
With a heavy heart
For he feels the hurt
As her lips quiver from the throbbing pain.
Unable to utter a word,
She blindly stares beyond his gaze
As if searching for an answer,
Within the showers of the pouring rain.

The roses he had given her
Now droop limply
In the vase on the table,
Their wilted petals now on the floor.
His vain attempt to heal the wounds
Had instead caused more sorrow and pain
Peeling the scabs from her wounded heart
That he knows he will never be able to cure.

Yet, they move on
Beyond this quiet, lonely room.
Sadly, they move on,
Without a kiss, a hug, or an embrace.
This was not how she had envisioned,
Not as she had hoped all along
As he turns and hesitantly walks out the door
While the tears continue to stream down her face.

Yet, the scars remain,
To be forever etched
On her wounded heart
Now aching with every troubled beat.
She screams, as the pain grows stronger,
And the hurt becomes more intense.
She watches him walk away, once more:
His bride to be, he is leaving to meet.

Morning...*for my son, Jamal*

Joyfully, a bananaquit chirps
As the sun climbs above the mountains.
Morning is awakening once again as slowly,
Another day dawns upon us.
Lazily, he rolls over in bed,
Just as the beautiful blooms spring to life,
Opening themselves to the bees and birds
Hovering expectantly above, seeking
Nectar, from within their stamens.

The Land Beckons Me

There is a land beckoning me.

I hear the sorrowful moans
From atop the mountains
Shedding its tears
As it rains, amid its pains,
Soothing the hurt that it feels,
Calming its worries and its fears.

There is a land beckoning me.

I hear the doleful cries
Of the rivers and streams,
As they slowly course along
And the sunbaked land cracks.
The crops slowly wither away,
While the long drought lingers on.

There is a land beckoning me.

I hear the shrill whistles
Of the birds, crying aloud with grief,
From atop the giant *Gommier* trees
Hoping the wind carries their message
To everyone in the distant lands
Who needs to hear their constant pleas.

There is a land beckoning me.

I hear the angry hiss
Bellowing from deep within its cavernous chambers
Spewing sulphuric steam,
Shrouding the desolate landscape
With a thick and eerie mist
That hovers menacingly over the crater's rim.

There is a land beckoning me.

I hear her calling
As the gentle waves roll in
Softly kissing the sandy shore.
She stays awake,
Enduring long and sleepless nights,
Hoping I will come walking through the door.

There is a land beckoning me.

I see the silvery light
Of the full moon, climbing majestically
Far beyond the darkened hills.
The rivers wind their way quickly
Along the deep valleys and gorges,
Slithering smoothly, as do conger eels.

There is a land beckoning me.

I hear the call of the land
Sadly beckoning me home,
While she nervously awaits my return.
I hear the sad and painful cry of the land,
As she looks to the flaming mountains
Where the raging fires continue to burn.

There is a land beckoning me.

Yes! I hear the groans of the land
As she beckons me home.
I feel the pain and long for the day,
When, to the Land, I shall return.
She will smile when that day comes,
Elated, that finally, I am there to stay.

There is a land beckoning me.

She will dance and jump with joy.
I will hear the rhythm of the *lapo kabwit*
Beat a steady, joyous refrain,
As the sound of the conch bellows loudly,
Signaling the return of a prodigal child.
The land will then smile amid its sorrow and pain.

There is a land beckoning me.

I will hear the voice of a people singing.
A people, singing with faith and in hope,
When the Land, her prize, has won.
She too, will chant and dance.
She will forget her pain and her sorrows, for a while,
As she welcomes home her long, lost son.

Yes! Dominica, beckons me home.

Hope

The sun now shines
Relieving the pain
And misery
Of the wretched storm.

Nightmare

He cowers on the cold, damp floor,
In the dark and lonely room.
Behind a heavy, bolted door
He contemplates his plight and doom.

His body wracks with pain:
His mind dances like fireflies in the night.
He screams aloud in vain
Wishing someone would show the light.

Worried about his own demise,
He wrestles with his mixed emotions.
Quietly he prays and hopes, he could rise,
Above this dark and miserable situation.

His body begins to quiver.
His heart strums against his chest
As everywhere seems to get darker:
Too scared is he, even to take a rest.

No one out there hears his pleas
Except the constant nagging flies
As he prays and pleads, on bended knees.
Yet useless it is, no matter how hard he tries.

Desperately, he attempts to rise,
Even if his frail body is very weak.
His captors pay no heed to his constant cries
Even though he hears them speak.

Sweat slowly streams to the floor
As he battles his growing fears
Desperately reaching for the door
Although he is blinded by the sweat and tears.

An eerie streak shines through tinted glass
Yet still, no one hears the calls,
Of a sorry, languishing and crumpled mass,
Now captive within these prison walls.

He hears his own loud thoughts
Echo against the thick, moldy walls.
Louder still, he wails and shouts
Hoping someone hears him down the hall.

He writhes in sheer agony and pain.
Screaming even louder and longer,
Yet sadly, it is all in vain
As his prison now appears to get smaller.

His bruised legs hurt
As he painfully creeps towards the door.
He has to stay alive and be alert
If he wants to escape the grasp of his captors.

However, he is too frail and weak.
His limbs now feel like lead.
He is weary, tired, confused, and sick
As pain hammers in his spinning head.

Yet, he wills himself to stand,
And attempts to grab unto the filthy walls.
But sadly, he cannot feel his hands,
And unto the cold, hard floor, he falls.

He feels the heavy darkness
Tighten its grasp around him like a vise
Rendering him weaker and helpless:
The pain and horror showing in his eyes.

“Is this real?” He screams in anger.
“Is this real or is it just a dream?”
Sadly, he gets no answer
No matter how loud he screams.

“Help me fight this horror!”
He prays to God once more.
Filled with desperation, he lunges for the door,
But, painfully, he lands unto the parquet floor.

The Letter

I received your letter today
That revealed all you had to say.
I got your letter today
Yet still, I am sorry you have walked away.

I got your letter today
Smeared with imprints of your tender lips.
I read your letter today
As your hurting heart painfully weeps.

I read your letter today
Since I could think of nothing else to do.
I read of your troubles today
And I know your pain is true.

I read your letter today.
I saw where your tears fell
Smudging the still wet ink
As your sad story, you tried to tell.

Your loving heart bleeds
While your beautiful body aches with pain.
I read of the hurt endured
Even, as you begin, a new life again.

I read your letter today, slowly,
As I stood alone on the water's edge
Wondering if the stories I heard are true
Though our love, to each other, we pledged.

Nevertheless, I tore that letter today, my dear,
Throwing the pieces into the rushing stream.
I watched as they sank and disappeared,
Like this long and haunted dream.

Goodbye then, my once dear one,
As I slowly walk along the narrow path,
Accompanied by the hissing insects,
Where in the moonlight, we use to kiss and laugh.

Goodbye, my darling dear, goodbye,
Even as the pain stifles my saddened heart,
For I have not name, nor riches, but love to give,
Yet sadly, someone has torn us apart.

The Church On The Hill

There is an old church on the hill
That looks upon the village.
A beacon of hope she was for anyone
Whom her help did seek.

Steadfast she always was,
Her doors open to everyone;
Lending comfort, peace, and hope,
To anyone who was tired, weak or sick.

On sunny days or in stormy weather
She stood firm, resolute, and strong.
A source of reassurance she was to all,
Whom her blessed help did crave.

A place of cheer on a Sunday morning
As the small, faithful congregation,
In song, worship, and praise,
Their thanks to God they willingly gave.

A place of peace, when all seemed lost,
Even in one's darkest hour.
A place of calm and serenity,
Even when violent storms raged outside.

Like a lighthouse upon the rock,
Her guiding light always shone.
A sign of comfort she always was,
To all who pained and cried.

However, today, she stands alone,
Her doors, now forever shut,
No more the place she was to all,
Because sadly, her demise, long ago began.

Her pastor, said his final goodbye
A sad, painful truth, for all to bear.
For his voice was stilled one Sunday morn,
Just at the break of dawn.

So tomorrow, we all will sadly watch,
As she is demolished.
For, soon, in her place, the people say,
A modern building will soon appear.

So, just for one last time, before they do,
Up that hill, I have to go.
There, on bended knees, I will say a prayer,
In honor of a church, so dear.

Moonlight

We walk in the park
In the calm
Of the night
As the full moon looks on.

Prisoner

Captive, behind a wall
Within this prison,
Of concrete, steel, and glass.
Walls thick, menacing, and tall,
Trying to get a reason
As I eagerly wait for time to pass.

I watch the sunset
Easing between the trees,
As the night slowly falls.
I am cold and wet,
Down on my hands and knees;
Trapped behind these imposing walls.

A future I seek
As time slowly marches on
To its own, mundane beat.
My body is tired and weak,
Yet, I continue to move on
This enemy I have to defeat.

My freedom I seek,
From the bars and walls,
Toiling tirelessly, all night.
I hear my captors speak
Yet they ignore my pleas,
My constant pain and my plight.

My legs are heavy like lead,
The reward, so evasive.
Nevertheless, I plod purposely along,
My eyes, focused ahead,
My ears, attentive,
Lest I slip and go wrong.

However, I stay the course
For I can't afford to waver
Even as I trip and fall.
No pity nor remorse
Now, more determined than ever,
As I answer the pleading call.

I continue to strive,
Purposeful and resolute,
A journey I have to finish.
A need to get to my goal alive,
Though frail and destitute;
Filled with pain and anguish.

Relentlessly, I journey on
To free myself of the pain
Seeping from these prison walls.
My freedom someday I will gain,
When I sing my sweet refrain,
Even as the darkness slowly falls.

Relentlessly, we journey on,
To free ourselves of the pain
Seeping from those prison walls.
Our freedom, someday we will win,
When we sing our sweet refrain,
Even as the darkness slowly falls.

Another Round

Dawn once again finds him,
Aimlessly walking the streets.
With no shoes on his swollen feet,
He searches for something to eat.

A trail of smoke hovers over his head
As he takes another long puff.
His loose, dirty denim pants
Dragging along the filthy street.

It has been another night outside
Sleeping in an abandoned house,
Even though he is not homeless.
To his family, now a disgrace.

Another day has dawned.
Now, along the street he walks
Unsteady his gait
Unkempt the beard, upon his face.

No liquor shops have opened,
Still too early, to do business.
He has a raging crave:
He needs a drink to start the day.

Therefore, up the hill he goes
A plea to make, once more.
The pain now unbearable;
He wonders what his wife will say.

He quickly reconsiders his plans
For he believes, it is better with his friends,
Till he gets drunk again, and unable,
To lift himself off the ground.

So the cycle continues, like always,
Beneath the aging mango tree,
Where they will gather again and wait,
Until someone makes another round.

Resurrection

The trees are all bare
But tomorrow
They all will see
The birds again.

The Migrant's Song

Like migratory birds
In the spring,
We head north,
Not going home,
But leaving home,
Abandoning everything,
And everyone;
Leaving siblings and parents,
Traversing the Atlantic,
As we go in search
Of a better life,
Chasing a dream.

From everywhere
We converge,
Seeking the *Eldorado,*
Seeking refuge
From our very own land;
Leaving what is behind
In the hands of caretakers.
Leaving our homes,
In search of money,
In search of jobs.
For our children,
A future, we try to carve.

In snow and sleet we trod,
In oppressive heat we toil,
To earn a living.
Unwanted strangers
In an unforgiving land.
Worried strangers,
Despised by some
In an envious, crime ridden,
And hostile neighborhood
Contrary to the *beautiful* picture
We once saw portrayed:
Now, so dark and grim.

Yet, we labor and we toil.
We struggle to survive and
To educate ourselves,
While holding to our values;
Values,
So true and deep.
We strive tirelessly,
To achieve our goals,
While clinging to
Our dreams and aspirations,
Regardless the cost;
For, that is all we have.

Giving up is not an option;
It never will be,
Because we know,
Only the weak and losers
Quit.
Yet, we work,
Amidst the violence, the hate, and the crime,
In the snow, the heat, and the filth.
We are like hostages
In a strange land
While the vultures lay in wait
For unsuspecting prey.

Our journey is sometimes
A long, scary, lonely one;
Yet still,
We forge gamely ahead
Bravely surmounting all obstacles,
In our way.
A mission
We have to accomplish
Till we get to the mountain top,
Even as the battle rages on
Within our souls
Amidst the pain and the tears.

Yet, we toil mercilessly,
By day and by night,
In darkness and in light.
We strive unerringly
For fairness,
Equality and justice.
We strive,
For an opportunity;
For a piece of the great dream,
That we have been chasing;
The dream that seems
To have slowly faded away.

Yet, like the birds all do,
We, too, shall wait
For our own winter
When, to warm lands,
Lands with food in abundance,
To feast on,
We shall fly.
There, to renew our faith,
Renew our belief,
In what we believe.
In what we hold dear,
As our own spring nears.

My Dominican Belle

Cadence music plays
In the background.
Darkness now covers the land
As I write,
Of the beauty and the charm,
The love and the pain,
The romance and the wonder,
That is you.
Oh beautiful child,
Standing out there in the rain,
Feeling the pain,
Bearing the hurt,
Feeling everything,
Yet, saying nothing.
You, my Dominican belle.
Crystal, pure water,
Cascading over your gentle body
As the sun shines upon your head.
You, with hair, long and black,
And the brown skin,
Or, is it the black skin?
However, who cares what skin it is?
So real and pure,
Smooth, sweet, and enticing.
Oh, beautiful one!
As you tantalizingly walk,
Along the black, sandy beach,
Dipping your toes
In the lapping waves
Of the placid Caribbean Sea,
Tormenting the hearts
Of the men, watching,

From the safety of the shadows,
Dreaming, wishing, and hoping
To hold you.
Oh, Dominican belle!
Nevertheless,
I write and I paint,
Your picture in my mind
Trying to remember what it looks like,
So I can transpose
The likeness of your image
To the bare canvas before me,
Trying to be true
To the person that you are.
For you are real,
My Dominican belle,
As I try to give you justice
With my hands and my eyes.
You, dressed in
The *madras*,
The *wob dwiyèt*,
The *tèt case*,
Or, walking alone,
Along the sandy beach,
In that captivating bikini:
You are whom you are.
A warm heart,
A cherished lover,
A gorgeous sister,
A beautiful hibiscus,
Freshly opened,
On a dew-laden morning.
You are,
A picture of love and life;
A picture of romance.
You, my Dominican belle!

The Snow

Sheets of fresh pure white
Coat the landscape
As the sun
Hides behind the clouds.

Dance, My Dear. Dance!

I stand aside and watch,
As everyone dances;
Slow, smooth, fast, and spirited,
As emotions run wild within their bodies.

I stand nervously and look
While the band plays.
Warm and smooth bodies
Slide easily, with every pulsating note.

I stand on the side in the dark,
Watching sweaty faces
Glow in the moonlight,
As dancers go through their paces.

They all move effortlessly,
Their eyes tightly closed,
As the moment overwhelms them.
Like butterflies, they quietly float.

Dance, my dear, dance!
Dance, until the sun rises in the morning.
Dance, and let the God of Love,
Arrest your racing heart.

I watch, as she dances alone.
I pray, fervently, for a chance
To hold her and spin her about;
Yet, I stand in the dark...alone.

She knows I am there,
For she teasingly looks my way
Wanting to banish the fear
That continues to keep us apart.

I am too scared to move,
Too scared to approach her,
As my heart races, uncontrollably;
Fear gripping my every bone.

I stare blankly from the dark,
Feeling myself drifting towards her,
As she smiles and glides towards me;
Then, in that moment, we become one.

We dance to our own music.
Just the two of us,
Even as the dance floor empties out.
Yes, we dance, as if we are in a trance.

We dance to our own rhythm,
Peering blankly, into each other's eyes.
We dance slowly to our own beat,
Hoping the fun would last until dawn.

Together we dance for one last time!
For someone will soon claim her heart
Stealing her away from me, again!
So, dance with me, my dear, dance!

Calypso Magic

Music blares.
Voices resound
From the stands,
As the batsman takes his guard.

The Last Dance

"One for the road," the bandsman cries.
"Hold on to the one you have.
Time to go home!" he shouts aloud.
"Those with no partner, please stand aside."

The bright lights slowly go dim
Signaling the end of the night
As the music plays, softly and slowly
While partners, across the floor, gently glide.

The melodies fill the festive night
While partners whisper softly
A word of love into each other's ear,
As the neon lights flicker off and on.

The feelings just now entrapping
Within each other's burning heart.
I don't believe it is time to go
For the party has only just begun.

Unexpectedly, the music stops.
We all stand, bewildered,
Wanting more, expecting more:
Yearning for that extra spin.

Yet still, we embrace our partners tightly
Fearful to let go for even a moment,
Lest we lose that sweet, yearning desire
That's been flowing so deep within.

The band strikes up again
To cheers and a thunderous roar.
Bodies gyrate provocatively and arms flail wildly,
As the band plays another song.

Come go home annou ale
Annou ale en kay mama nous
Come go home annou ale
Annou ale en kay mama nous

We join in the melodious refrain
As the other dancers swarm the floor,
Their sweaty bodies going wild
Enjoying the moment; having fun.

Someone dims the lights once again.
Hoarse voices scream out aloud,
The sound echoing in the distance
As we dance in our own way.

We hold unto each other and dance.
We jump and prance...wildly.
The crescendo in the room heightens
As we sing aloud, the sweet *lavway*.

Colorful skirts swirl loftily
Over the heads of partners.
Women gyrate provokingly
Across the floor…smooth and slick.

We dance, as the roosters crow repeatedly.
We dance as dogs bark and donkeys bray,
Joining the early morning celebration,
As if playing their own cadence music.

The music slows down
And stops for the last time,
Tantalizingly, as we wait,
Hoping for one more tune.

"It's time my dear," I whisper
As she embraces me tenderly
For she wants to keep dancing
In the bright light, of the silvery moon.

Therefore, we dance one last dance:
Just the two of us,
Along the water's edge,
As the waves roll in quietly.

We dance to our own music
Leaving our footprints in the wet sand,
And the crescent moon smiles
While we dance! Slowly!

The Sun Rises Tomorrow

Wé papa!
Mi déba!
Oh brother!
Oh sister!
I watch
Mystified
As pen and paper
Talk eerily, to each other.

Who is in charge?
Whom should we call?
Who has a story to tell
As we begin to grow old
Yet strive bravely
Even as we pine for sunny days of yesterday
When we were brash and bold?

Who is insecure out there?
Who needs a cure today?
Who needs a word of courage,
In their darkest hour?
Be real to each other
Even if we hear the useless chatter
It is still a wonderful world
With all its awe and wonder.

Today. Yes, today,
Was just another day
Filled with many hopes and dreams
As I tried picking up the countless pieces.
Feverishly, I searched for the light
That would show the way.
But sadly, today is gone,
Just like those elusive, dreamy wishes.

It is tough.
It is rough.
I hear myself screaming,
Screaming even louder.
Nevertheless, there is a light ahead.
No, it is not a witch riding
On a broken broomstick.
It is the light of hope, my brother.

The night begins to roll in
As day slowly takes its leave.
A brisk cool breeze blows west,
While somewhere, a *sikiyay* sings.
The dreams for today have died
Yet, I eagerly wait for tomorrow,
To see the rising sun,
And the hope that it brings.

I Hear Your Cries

Oh Dominica! I hear your constant cries.
I hear your deep, mournful sighs.
I see the tears of anguish, slowly flowing,
As your children's voices, in the dark, keep calling.

I hear the painful moans, ripping you apart.
I feel the words stabbing at your bleeding heart
As you struggle daily, to remain loyal and faithful,
Even to those, so cruel, treacherous, and revengeful.

I hear you, my Dominica! My Waitukubuli!
I hear your pleas, as on your knees, you beg for mercy,
Interceding, on behalf of your children held hostage,
By those who plunder, rape, murder, and pillage.

I hear the bells ringing atop the verdant mountains,
Beseeching us all, to gather again, even as it rains.
I hear the *Siffleur Montagne* sing with the rushing rivers,
Begging us all, our cold, hardened hearts, to surrender.

I see the pain chiseled deeply, upon your troubled face,
As many, choose to turn and run away, in disgrace,
Forgetting where you have been, and whom you are:
A nation of the children of Jacko, Bala, and Mabouya.

Oh Dominica! Yes, I feel the never-ending pains,
As the dishonest among us, acquire fraudulent gains,
While the dissenters, your innocent image smear,
With no cause for concern, worry, reproach, or fear.

I cry, too, as your resplendent beauty is marred.
I weep, too, as your fragile and tender body is scarred,
Poisoned daily by spite, malice, hatred, envy, and deceit.
Darkened by theft, greed, selfishness, treason, and conceit.

Oh! Cry my Dominica! Cry, for your wilted flowers.
Cry, for your misguided sons and whoring daughters.
Weep, my Dominica! Weep out of desperation,
Moreover, let your constant tears heal this broken nation.

Yes Dominica! I cry with you, my island dear,
And I, too, sadly and uncontrollably, shed many a tear,
As I bow my aching head, in sadness and in shame,
While politicians battle for power, in your name.

But, weep no more! Dear land, so young and fair,
Weep no more, in shame and out of despair.
Stand strong and confident, my dear beloved nation;
Be steadfast and resolute, in the midst of the confusion.

Weep not, because of your green, towering mountains.
Weep not because of your rugged and unforgiving terrain.
Be steadfast! Stand strong! Be resolute. Be brave!
Rejoice; for many, daily, your beauty they do crave.

Weep not, thou Land of natural, exquisite beauty.
Weep no more my beloved Waitukubuli.
Weep not, dear Land of the proud and majestic Sisserou.
Weep not, oh Dominica! To thyself, O Land be true.

Let all the dissenters who are quick to do you harm,
Those who abuse your innocence and your charm,
Now kneel before you in remorse and humility,
Seeking your forgiveness and pardon, with sincerity.

Let not the wicked tongue of the vile subservient,
Force you to become timid, coy, scared, and silent,
Nor, let it cause you to cower meekly in fright,
Instead, get up Dominica! Get up! Get up and fight!

However, let all who love and cherish you stand together,
As we fight poverty, ignorance, *mepuis,* and slander;
Let all who love you, protect you my dear,
Against the armies of injustice, confusion, hatred, and fear.

Let us your children, your marred innocence reclaim!
Let us, in one accord, speak of your once great acclaim!
Let us your simplicity of life once again regain!
Let us, your modesty, purity, and virginity, strive to maintain!

So, weep not, oh Diablotin! Weep not, oh Sisserou!
Weep not Jacko, Pharcels, Mabouya, Balla, and Cicero,
For tomorrow morning, to the east, our eyes shall face,
As a new hopeful day, dawns on this blessed place.

Yes, we shall give our thanks to Him, who reigns,
As together, we gather as one, atop the mountains,
Where we will raise our voices up high, in one accord,
As we lift you up, giving all the thanks to our God.

They will resound over the verdant hills and deep valleys.
Over the flowing rivers, pristine lakes, and dark gullies.
They will resound again throughout the villages and hamlets,
Through the turquoise bays and your hidden inlets.

So weep not, Waitukubuli! Rather, rejoice.
Weep not, Dominica! Please, listen to my voice.
Weep, no more, Dominica, for the dawn approaches,
As the soft, golden rays brighten up your sandy beaches.

You owe nothing to anyone my island dear,
For you are not the one who has been bitter and insincere.
Hang not your head in shame, nor in disgrace.
Lift up thy head and proudly show your gentle face.

Pa pléwé Donmnik mwen, pa helay
Chenbe for! Peyi mwen! Pa pléwé
For surely the day shall come,
When your children quell this turbulent storm.

Pa pléwé, payi a mwen! Pa pléwé.
Pa pléwé Donmnik mwen. Pa plewe!

Like Crabs In A Barrel

Like crabs in a barrel
We pull each other down.
Our brother's successes
We treat with disdain and scorn.

Like a rushing river
We carry away all in our path.
Like hyenas we laugh
At each other's innocent gaff.

Like starving lions in a den
At each other we ravenously tear.
Spewing discord, malice, and hatred,
Our sister's name we are quick to smear.

Oh! How sad the way we have become!
No longer are we a village.
How cruel, cold, and heartless,
As we destroy, hurt, and pillage.

Being gentle and being kind,
We now sadly frown upon.
"Hello, hi, how do you do?"
We treat with disdain and with scorn.

Oh, where are we heading?
Where are we going?
Who is at the helm?
Who is doing the sailing?

On a ship adrift in rough, turbulent seas,
We are heading to our own destruction.
The crew we have thrown overboard,
Making us victims of our own creation.

The darkness nears and thunder roars,
As we fervently pray to God for help.
Though still immersed in our drunken stupor,
Like trapped dogs, we now growl and yelp.

Yes, we are like crabs in a barrel
Pulling each other down,
Treating each other,
With disdain and scorn!

Coward

Coward!

He hides in the dark
Patiently waiting
For an unwary victim
To assault and to rob her
Of her dignity,
Of her womanhood,
Her self-worth,
As he creates fear and inflicts pain.

Coward!

Filled with anger
He desperately walks
The crowded street
Seeking a naïve pedestrian to rob
Among the busy crowd
Taking away his possession
In order to satisfy his sick obsession.
Oh what a coward! So vile and vain!

Coward!

He stalks his victim
Intently watching
Her every step
From his secret hideout.
He preys on her fragility and innocence
Stealing her virginity,
Causing hurt and shame
As he commits another brutal rape.

Coward!

Awake all night
Silently scouring
Our peaceful neighborhoods
While we sleep
Pilfering and destroying
Satisfying his inner cravings
With no guilt nor misgivings,
As in the dark, he makes his escape.

Coward!

So remorseless,
Bold, and cold-hearted;
He intimidates his victims.
With sheer disregard for life,
He continually abuses
Innocent, defenseless children,
Filling their parents' hearts
With anger, sorrow, and life-long pain.

Coward!

He kills callously,
Lives recklessly,
Snatching our precious ones:
Our dear children,
Before we get to know them.
He robs us of the chance
To enjoy those precious moments
All for his own sick and selfish gain.

Coward!

A cold-hearted,
Guiltless and stone-faced monster,
Hiding behind a mask.
Preying
On the sick and elderly,
Creating fear and causing panic,
Among the helpless
As he wrecks dreams and promising lives.

He is a coward,
Waiting patiently,
To spring,
Like an animal of prey,
Smothering precious lives.
He humiliates and traumatizes
Unsuspecting victims
With his hands, guns and knives.

Coward! Yes. He is a coward!

My Four Seasons

Winter,
My butt I freeze.
Spring,
It makes me sneeze.
Summer,
It is too darn hot.
Fall
Way too short.
However, that brings me back to
Winter-Spring-Summer-Fall.
I guess I will have to give
Mother Nature a call.
Yet I doubt I will get through to her,
Since her voice box must be full by now,
For everyone has been calling her.
They are unhappy and creating a row.

Atop The Mountain

I am not here to gossip,
Nor am I here to be hip.
I am not here to spy,
Nor am I here to lie.

I am not here to demean,
Nor am I here to be mean.
I am not here to criticize,
Nor am I here to chastise.

I am not here to break down,
Nor am I here to take down.
I am not here to gloat,
Nor to be anyone's scapegoat.

I am not here to satisfy your urges,
Nor be victim of your grudges.
I am not here to be an illusion,
Nor to suffer from your retaliation.

I am here, so I may share.
I am here, because I care.
I am here, because I know,
To dodge your poisoned arrow.

I am here, whether you want, or not.
I am here, whether you grunt, or not.
I am here, whether it rains, or not.
I am here, whether it pains, or not.

I am here, to entertain and create.
I am here, to help and educate.
I am here, to show the light,
In the dark, lonely hours of the night.

I am here, because of God's will.
No, not because of the way you feel.
I am here, because God planned it.
I am here, because he saw it fit.

I am here, because I am me.
I am here, because he set me free.
I am here, because there is hope:
Hope, so with your crap, I may cope.

I am here! Yes! I am here!
However, I will not shed a single tear,
Lest you think, I am frail and weak.
Brother, my deeds for me shall speak.

Because brother! I am here!
Breathing the fresh, pure air.
Here, where the cool wind blows.
Here, where the clear water flows.

I am here my angry brother.
I am here my pained sister.
I am here, atop the majestic mountains,
Bathed by the clear, cool, refreshing rains.

I am where you cannot hurt me.
I am here, where all I see,
Is anger, prejudice, and disdain,
Flowing through your poisoned veins.

Nonetheless, I am here, enjoying the beauty,
While you sulk in your vanity.
I am here, this wonderful view to enjoy,
While a way, my being you seek to destroy.

Nevertheless, I am here! Oh, what a sight!
I am here! In the stillness of the night,
Enjoying the beautiful moonlight.
Just me…atop my mountain tonight!

Arise Dominica

What is freedom of speech?
What is freedom anyhow?
What does it mean to be free?
Where does it start and end?
When does it stop or end?
Can someone please tell me?

Does it mean to slander?
Does it mean to despise?
Does it mean to smear?
Is there a set limit?
Is there a stop sign ahead?
Is it okay to rip, mutilate, and tear?

Are we heading up?
Are we heading down?
Are we going nowhere?
As our politicians sow division
That our people naively cultivate,
Spreading malice, hate, anger, and fear.

From our hearts, we grow venom
From our mouths, we spew discord.
While our thoughts are corrupted by envy and greed.
Distrust, we spread about like seeds,
As anger, spite, and wickedness,
Our beings we constantly feed.

Isn't it time for us to pause?
Isn't it time to kneel and pray?
Time to harness our runaway anger?
It is time to heal our wounded nation
Time to seek peace and unity
Time to respect each other.

Blue, green, red, black, or white
What does it really matter?
While the nation sinks slowly,
Overloaded with our malaise and sins.
The leaders ridiculed, beaten, and spat on,
While we despise the shut-in and elderly.

The uneducated among us grow foolish,
While the wise deceive us daily.
The honest we reject, scorn, and shame,
While the hardworking ones we beat and rob.
Our island nation groans loudly,
As, sadly, we smear her sacred name.

Where have we gone wrong?
Where do we lay the blame?
Is it the school, the church, or the media?
We need to heal the bleeding wounds,
Lest they become septic,
And in time, we all perish together.

Oh Dominica! My heart pains and grieves,
My stomach churns and rumbles,
As I see the sad and painful plight,
Of an ill-disciplined, narrow-minded people,
Lost and adrift on stormy seas,
On a dark, cold, and lonely night.

They pray fervently for the morning,
Yet, the one at the helm, they curse.
Desperate and facing a long and dreary night
They wail and groan, out of fear and hunger.
"Help!" they cry out aloud! "Help!" they scream,
Now worried and scared, as they see no land in sight.

Wake up people! Wake up my fellow Dominicans!
Shake yourselves free brothers.
Sister, shake loose the chains,
Of hatred, anger, greed, and slander.
Shake loose the shackles of discord and
The heavy chains of selfishness and disdain.

Stop aiming at each other's throat.
Stop turning our backs on the creator.
Stop, now, the shame and humiliation.
Rather, rise up my People! Rise! Rise!
Rise up together, as a united Dominica.
Rise up Dominicans, and save our Nation!

They Come

They come,
Bearing gifts and empty promises.
They all come,
Playing on the hunger of the masses.

They come,
Their pockets filled with deceit.
They all come,
Soon to beat a hasty retreat.

They come,
Each one, his goal to achieve,
No matter the cost;
While the people struggle to live.

With flags waving
And asking for love and peace,
They come, riding into town,
Singing their anthems of injustice.

With smiles and kisses,
They win over the poor and weak.
Yet, in the moment of truth,
On our behalf, they fail to speak.

Therefore, like colors they regard us:
Not as people anymore,
But like chips in a pawn game,
Hoping they get a winning score.

Yet, our dear nation moans,
As it suffers and cries,
As it groans and aches,
From the ill-will, deceit, and lies.

Once, a nation so pure and clean,
Now soiled and defamed,
By her children's own devious deeds,
As they seek power, money, and fame.

Their very own they distrust.
The enemy, they eye in disgust.
Yet, they come bearing gifts,
Pleading with us to win their trust.

Like vultures circling beneath the clouds,
They wait their time patiently,
To pounce on the unsuspecting,
With beaks and claws, strong and deadly.

However, they all come,
Wearing colors of red, blue, and green,
By day and night; in rain or shine,
While a sad, deceived people, cry within.

Yet, they come!
Yes, they come hoping.
Still, they come
While the people, keep hurting.

Yes, they come!

What Do You Do?

What do you do
When the mind tells you
To get up
But the body says
You should not?
What do you do
As the cold wind blows
And impatience grows?
You have things to do,
Heights to achieve:
Yet,
You doubt your emotions,
For something has to give.
Stay in! Go out!
Wake up! Stay here!
The guilt stands before you,
Like a mirror
Reflecting your thoughts,
While time moves along.
The clock
On the bare wall
Goes
Ding, dong, ding, dong,
Like a song,
That plays in your head.
You have a task ahead
To accomplish.
A mission to complete.
Yet, even if you wish,
There is nothing
You can achieve
Without you at the helm.
So, whether it's cold;

Whether it is hot,
Whether it is stormy,
Whether the weather,
Is brutal or balmy,
No matter how you feel,
Out you go.
In the ice and snow,
Sun or rain,
Heat or cold,
Or, even as the wind
And driving rain,
Whip against your face.
For you know,
No one reaches the mountaintop,
Unless he begins the journey,
No matter how long,
Or how short,
With one single step at the base.
So body, come along!
Follow the mind,
Lest you are left behind.

Living In Hope

Dusk approaches slowly,
And leaves fall quietly
To the ground,
While from up high,
The birds whistle their tunes:
A sweet melodious sound.

The wind softly whispers,
Through the trees.
The branches slowly sway
Back and forth,
As animals seek shelter
From the darkness and their prey.

The church bells resound,
As the aging sexton
Dutifully signals six o'clock
Slow and methodical,
Like he has always done
For the village's faithful flock.

Mothers, in the village, grow restless,
As their children
Reluctantly stop their ring games,
Responding slowly and grudgingly
To their mothers' pleas,
Now screaming aloud their names.

The waves roll in quietly,
Lapping on the shore.
Small crabs, scouring the sand
For something to eat,
Beat a hasty retreat,
Seeking refuge on dry land.

The sun slips quietly
Beneath the horizon
Leaving a soft, green glow
As it slowly inches from sight.
And we live in hope,
To see it rise again tomorrow.

GIFTUS 2014

A Geejay Arts Production-2015
Giftus R. John
http://www. geejayartsandphoto.com
908-370-7760